I'M ALLERGIC TO STRAWBERRIES

By Maria Nelson

Gareth Stevens
PUBLISHING

Please visit our website, www.garethstevens.com. For a free color catalog of all our high-quality books, call toll free 1-800-542-2595 or fax 1-877-542-2596.

Library of Congress Cataloging-in-Publication Data

Nelson, Maria.
I'm allergic to strawberries / by Maria Nelson.
p. cm. — (I'm allergic)
Includes index.
ISBN 978-1-4824-0985-7 (pbk.)
ISBN 978-1-4824-0986-4 (6-pack)
ISBN 978-1-4824-0984-0 (library binding)
1. Food allergy in children — Juvenile literature. 2. Strawberries — Juvenile literature.
I. Nelson, Maria. II. Title.
RJ386.5 N45 2014
618.92—d23

Published in 2015 by
Gareth Stevens Publishing
111 East 14th Street, Suite 349
New York, NY 10003

Designer: Nicholas Domiano
Editor: Kristen Rajczak

Photo credits: Cover, p. 1 Betsie Van Der Meer/Taxi/Getty Images; pp. 3–24 (background texture), 5 © iStockphoto.com/SolStock; p. 7 Angela Aladro mella/ Shutterstock.com; p. 9 moodboard/Thinkstock.com; p. 11 Levent Konuk/ Shutterstock.com; p. 13 cowardlion/Shutterstock.com; p. 15 mario loiselle/E+/ Getty Images; p. 17 arek_malang/Thinkstock.com; p. 19 llaszio/Shutterstock.com; p. 21 lsantilli/Shutterstock.com.

Printed in the United States of America

CPSIA compliance information: Batch #CS15GS: For further information contact Gareth Stevens, New York, New York at 1-800-542-2595.

Contents

Fantastic Fruit. 4

What's the Cause?. 6

The Reaction 8

Epinephrine 14

Other Fruit Allergies. 16

Stay Away!. 20

Glossary. 22

For More Information 23

Index 24

Boldface words appear in the glossary.

Fantastic Fruit

Fruits are some of the best foods you can eat. They're healthy for you and taste good, too! Not everyone can eat all fruits, though. Some people are **allergic** to strawberries!

What's the Cause?

Strawberry allergies happen because of a **protein** in the fruit. The body **identifies** the protein as harmful. It creates special parts of the blood called antibodies to fight the protein.

7

The Reaction

Once the body has sent antibodies after the strawberry proteins, an allergic **reaction** occurs. This commonly happens about 1 to 2 hours after someone with a strawberry allergy has eaten strawberries or something containing strawberries.

Some common allergic reactions to strawberries are **swelling** and a burning feeling around or in the mouth. Your throat might feel tight, and your skin may become itchy and red, too.

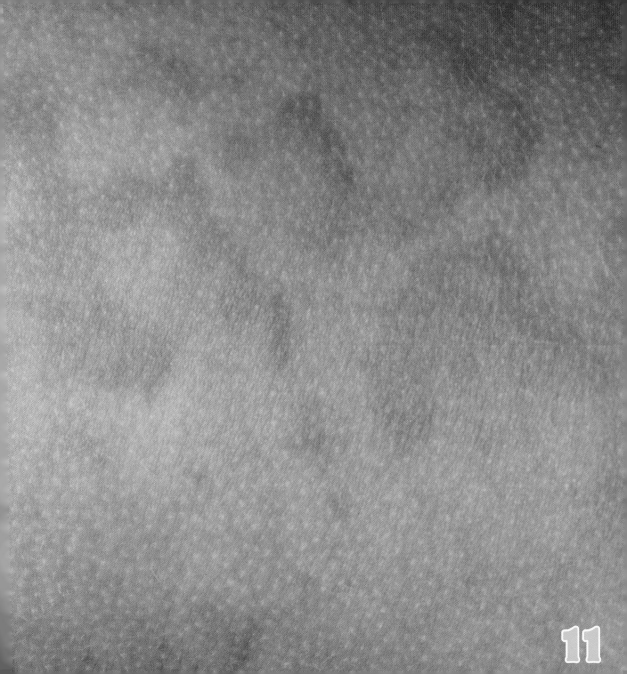

Allergic reactions to strawberries can also include tummy aches and throwing up. The most serious reaction is called anaphylaxis (aa-nuh-fuh-LAK-suhs). Someone with anaphylaxis may have trouble breathing and even pass out.

13

Epinephrine

Common allergic reactions can be treated with drugs you buy at the store. Worse reactions, such as anaphylaxis, need a shot of drug called epinephrine (eh-puh-NEH-fruhn). Some people with bad allergies carry their own shot!

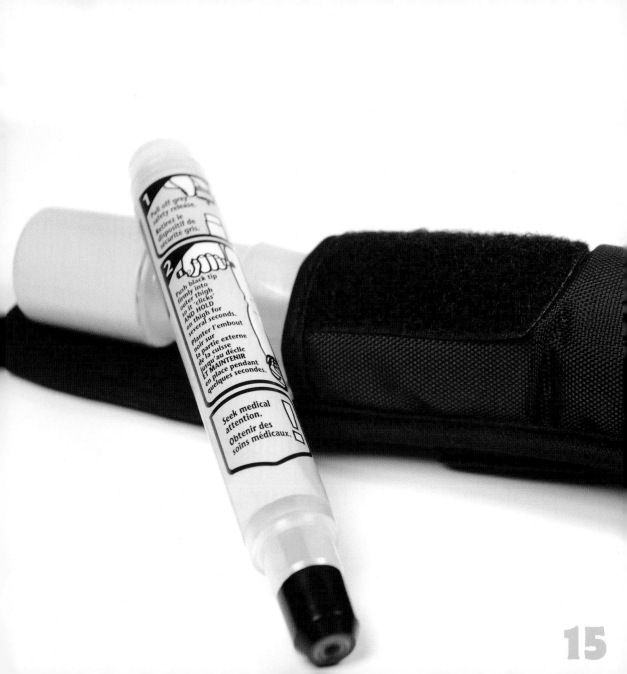

1 Pull off grey safety release.
Retirez le dispositif de sécurité gris.

2 Push black tip firmly into outer thigh so it 'clicks' AND HOLD on thigh for several seconds.
Planter l'embout noir sur la partie externe de la cuisse jusqu'au déclic ET MAINTENIR en place pendant quelques secondes.

Seek medical attention.
Obtenir des soins médicaux.

15

Other Fruit Allergies

Strawberries aren't the only fruit someone could be allergic to! Apples, bananas, and melons are just a few more. Allergic reactions to these fruits are also caused by proteins found in them.

Pollen can be the cause of allergic reactions to fruit, too. Plant pollen can be found on certain fruits. If someone is allergic to that kind of plant pollen, it would seem as if they were reacting to the fruit.

Stay Away!

If you're allergic to strawberries, the only way to keep from having an allergic reaction is to stay away from strawberries! That means no strawberry jam, strawberry ice cream, or strawberry shortcake.

21

Glossary

allergic: having a sensitivity to usually harmless things in the surroundings, such as dust, pollen, or foods

identify: recognize

pollen: a fine yellow dust produced by plants

protein: one of the main building blocks of the body

reaction: a response

swelling: to grow larger in an uncommon way

For More Information

Books

Glaser, Jason. *Food Allergies*. Mankato, MN: Capstone Press, 2007.

Gordon, Sherri Mabry. *Are You at Risk for Food Allergies? Peanut Butter, Milk, and Other Deadly Threats*. Berkeley Heights, NJ: Enslow Publishers, Inc., 2014.

Websites

Food Allergies
kidshealth.org/kid/ill_injure/sick/food_allergies.html
On this site just for kids, read about the many kinds of food allergies and how they can affect your life.

Food Allergy Research and Education
www.foodallergy.org/resources/kids
Learn more about your food allergy so you can teach your friends and family about it, too!

Index

anaphylaxis 12, 14
antibodies 6, 8
apples 16
bananas 16
burning feeling 10
drugs 14
epinephrine 14
itchy 10
melons 16
pollen 18
protein 6, 8, 16
swelling 10
throwing up 12
trouble breathing 12
tummy aches 12